Swim, Climb, and Fly

MW00808522

Written by Jill Eggleton

Rigby

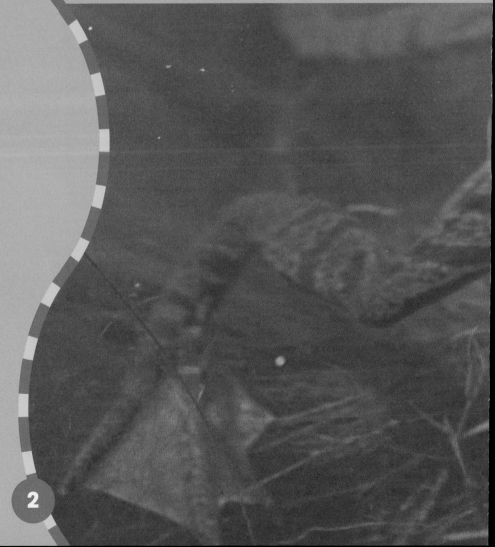

Look!
This frog can swim.

2

This lizard can swim.

Look! Look!
This frog can climb.

6

This lizard can climb.

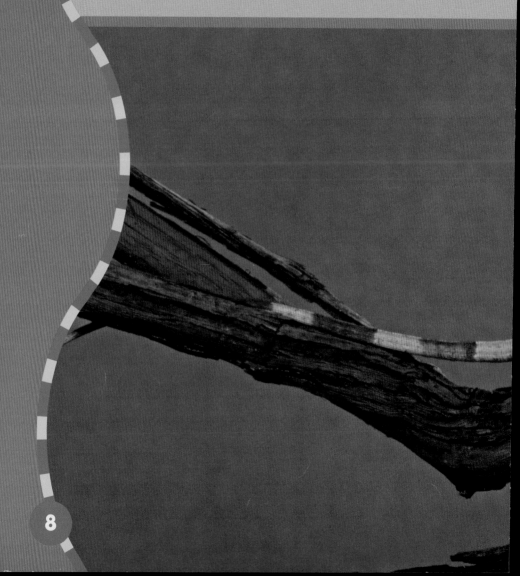

Look! Look! Look!
This frog can fly.

This lizard can fly!

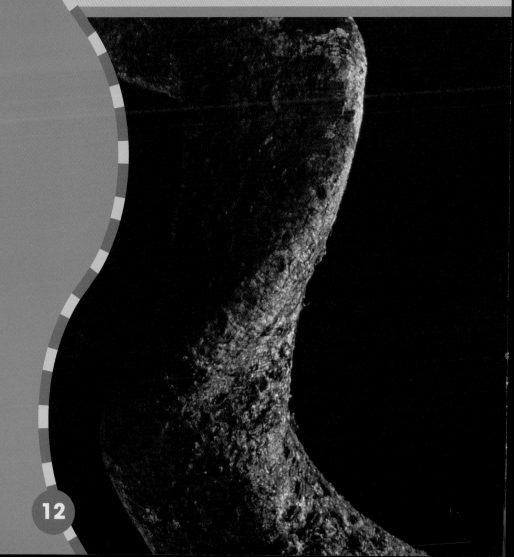

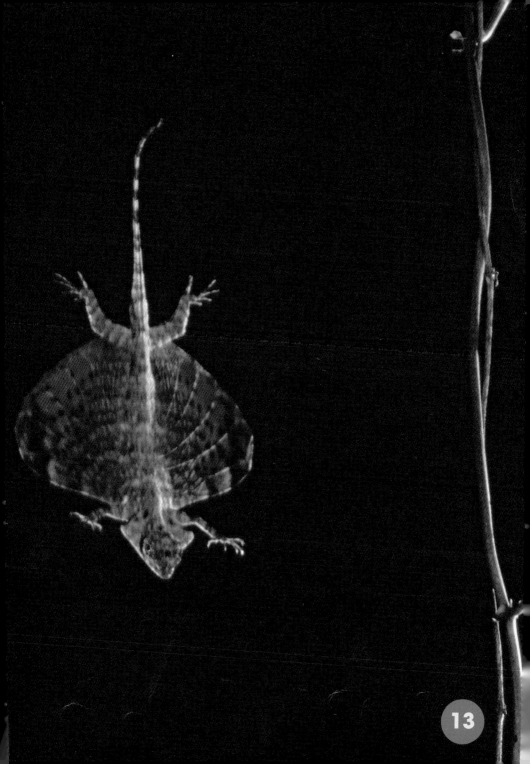

Guide Notes

Title: Swim, Climb, and Fly

Stage: Emergent – Magenta

Genre: Nonfiction (Expository)

Approach: Guided Reading

Processes: Thinking Critically, Exploring Language, Processing Information

Written and Visual Focus: Photographs (static images), Index, Labels

FORMING THE FOUNDATION

Tell the children that this book is about two animals that can swim, climb, and fly.
Talk to them about what is on the front cover. Read the title and the author.
Focus the children's attention on the index and talk about the actions.
"Walk" through the book, focusing on the photographs and talk about what the frogs and lizards can both do.

Read the text together.

THINKING CRITICALLY

(sample questions)

After the reading
- What do you think might be the difference between a frog that can fly and a frog that can swim?
- Where do you think a lizard and a frog might fly to?

EXPLORING LANGUAGE

(ideas for selection)

Terminology
Title, cover, author, photographs

Vocabulary
Interest words: frog, lizard, fly, swim
High-frequency words: this, look, can